*c.*750 BC	Celts from Hallstatt (in present-day Austria) trade salt with the Ancient Greeks. Celtic civilisation gradually spreads out along the rivers Rhine and Danube
500 BC	By this date, Celtic civilisation is firmly established in Britain
225 BC	The Romans defeat the Celts at the battle of Telamon and start to take control of the Celtic lands in mainland Europe
55 BC	The Roman general, Julius Caesar, invades Britain with 10,000 soldiers, but does not conquer the country as he had hoped
54 BC	Caesar tries once more to conquer Britain, but fails again
AD 43	The Roman emperor, Claudius, sends an army to invade Britain
49-50	The Celtic leader Caratacus fights back against the Romans. He is finally defeated in AD 51
60	Boudicca, the queen of the Iceni, leads a revolt against the Romans, but is defeated
122	Hadrian's Wall is built across the north of England to give protection from Celtic raiders from further north
143	The Antonine Wall is built from the Clyde to the Forth, but is abandoned after about 20 years
200	Christianity starts to spread in Britain after this date. Its followers are persecuted by the Romans

270	The first Saxon raiders threaten to attack Britain
312	The Roman emperor Constantine becomes a Christian and soon makes Christianity the official religion of the Roman Empire
367	Saxons attack Britain but are defeated
385	Saint Patrick is probably born in this year
402	The last of the Roman armies leave Britain to go and defend Rome. Angles, Jutes and Saxons continue their raids on the south and east of Britain
450	Irish Celts invade the west of mainland Britain, while Celts from what are now Cornwall and Devon go to settle in Brittany. At the same time, the Angles, Jutes and Saxons start to settle in eastern Britain
664	The Celtic Church joins with the Roman Church and accepts the Pope in Rome as its leader
793	Viking raids start with an attack on the monastery at Lindisfarne
1014	Brian Boru, king of Ireland, defeats the Vikings at the battle of Clontarf
1066	William, Duke of Normandy, invades England and becomes king. The Celtic way of life continues in Ireland, and much of Scotland and Wales

BRITAIN THROUGH THE AGES

Celts

Hazel Mary Martell

Evans Brothers Limited

First published by
Evans Brothers Limited
2A Portman Mansions
Chiltern St
London W1U 6NR

Reprinted 2006, 2010

Printed in China

British Cataloguing in Publication Data
Martell, Hazel Mary
The Celts. – (Britain Through the ages)
Celts – Great Britain – Juvenile literature 2. Great
Britain – History – To 55 B.C.- Juvenile literature
I.Title
936. 1'02
ISBN 978 0 237 52575 0

Acknowledgements
Design: Ann Samuel
Editorial: Nicola Barber
Illustrations: Nick Hawken
Production: Jenny Mulvanny

Acknowledgements

For permission to reproduce copyright material,
the author and publishers gratefully acknowledge
the following:

Cover (main) Werner Forman Archive (back-
ground) The Bridgeman Art Library
(top) © Skyscan Balloon Photography/English
Heritage Photo Library
(middle & bottom) The Ancient Art & Architecture
Collection. Title page British Museum,
London/Werner Forman Archive. Contents page
A.Baggett/Ancient Art & Architecture Collection
Ltd. page 7 (top) English Heritage Photographic
Library. page 9 (top) R. Sheridan/The Ancient Art
& Architecture Collection, (bottom) Dorset Natural
History & Archaeological Society/Werner Forman
Archive. page 10 British Museum,
London/Werner Forman Archive. page 11 (top left
and right) British Museum, London/Werner
Forman Archive, (bottom) Musée Archaeologique
de Breteuil/ Werner Forman Archive. page 12
British Museum, London/The Bridgeman Art
Library. page 13 (left) R.Sheridan/The Ancient Art
& Architecture Collection. page 14 (top)
Chesterfield Borough Council Recreation and
Leisure Dept., (bottom) R.Sheridan/The Ancient
Art & Architecture Collection. page 15
R.Sheridan/The Ancient Art & Architecture
Collection. page 16 R.Sheridan/The Ancient Art &
Architecture Collection. page 17 (top)
R.Sheridan/The Ancient Art & Architecture
Collection, (bottom) National Museum of
Scotland. page 18 British Museum,
London/Werner Forman Archive. page 19 Skyscan
Balloon Photography/English Heritage Photo
Library, (top right) Paul Birkbeck/ English
Heritage Photo Library, (bottom) Cheryl
Hogue/The Ancient Art & Architecture Collection.
page 20 Peter Clayton. page 21
R.Sheridan/Ancient Art & Architecture Collection.
page 22 English Heritage Photo Library. page 23
(top) Skyscan Balloon Photography/English
Heritage Photo Library, (bottom) R.Sheridan/The
Ancient Art & Architecture Collection. page 24
John P.Stevens/The Ancient Art & Architecture
Collection. page 25 R.Sheridan/The Ancient Art &
Architecture Collection, (bottom) British Library,
London/The Bridgeman Art Library. page 27 (top
left) Philip Craven/Robert Harding Picture
Library, (top right) Ortak Jewellery Ltd., (bottom)
Cadw/Welsh Historic Monuments. page 28 Trinity
College, Dublin/The Bridgeman Art Library. page
29 (top) City of Bristol Museum & Art Museum,
(bottom) 25 R.Sheridan/The Ancient Art &
Architecture Collection.

Contents

A part of Celtic Europe

The people we call the Celts are first heard of in the 8th century BC. We know that they mined salt at Hallstatt in present-day Austria. They traded the salt with their neighbours, and they also crossed the Alps to trade with the Ancient Greeks. The Greeks called them *Keltoi*, which was probably similar to the name they called themselves.

As well as being miners, these early Celts were farmers and metalworkers. They knew how to make weapons and tools from iron. The Celts' iron tools were stronger than any used before in that part of Europe. Using these tools, the Celts cleared more land and grew more crops. As they produced more food, the population increased. Soon, groups of Celts began to move out along the rivers Rhine and Danube in search of new lands. By the 6th century BC, Celtic civilisation had spread west to France, Belgium, Spain, Portugal and the British Isles. It had also spread east into the Balkans and parts of Turkey, as well as across central Europe and into the valley of the River Po in northern Italy.

This map shows how far Celtic civilisation had spread by the 2nd century BC. It also shows where the main Celtic tribes lived.

Words, words, words...

Some modern-day place names are based on the names of Celtic tribes. Paris is called after the Parisii, and Belgium after the Belgae. The Swiss call their country Helvetia, after the Helvetii who used to live there.

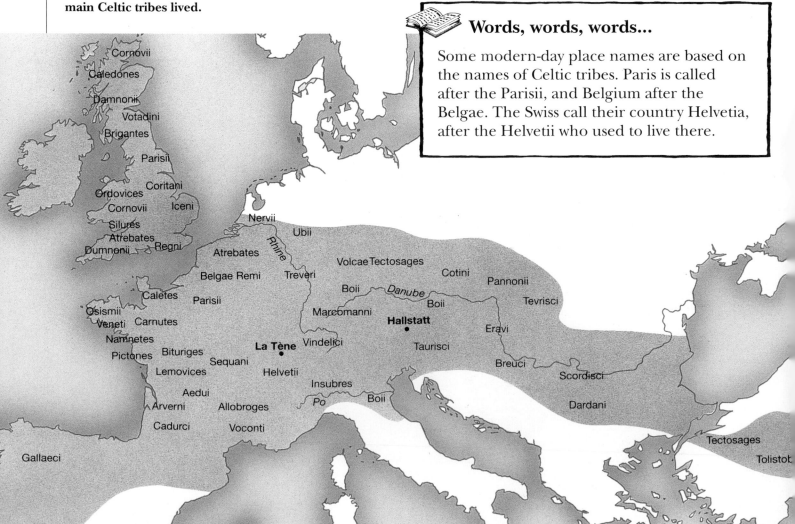

Many different tribes

No matter where they settled, different groups of Celts still had a lot in common. They spoke versions of the same language and had the same ways of life. But they were never united under one ruler. Instead they remained in different tribes, each with its own name and its own territory. Sometimes these tribes went to war with each other, at other times they fought together against a common enemy.

Scientific evidence now suggests that this figure of a horse was cut into the hillside in Oxfordshire before Celtic times, but the Celts with their love of horses kept it in good repair.

Barbarians

Unlike the Ancient Greeks and Romans, the Celts did not build towns and cities with grand public buildings and fine temples. Instead they lived in small villages and farmsteads scattered around the countryside. The Romans thought that the Celts were uncivilised and called them 'barbarians'. In fact, the Celts were skilled craftworkers who sent many of their goods to be sold in Rome. They also had a system of looking after the poor, the old and the sick which was far more advanced than any similar system in the Roman world.

It's true!

In the days before people had refrigerators, salt was used to stop meat from going bad if it was not going to be eaten straight away.

How do we know?

The early Celts did not write anything down, but we know about them from books written by the Ancient Greeks and Romans who traded and fought with them. Throughout this book you will find comments from some of these writers.

We also know a lot from the work of archaeologists who excavate (dig up) sites where the Celts lived. Archaeologists study the objects they find to tell us what everyday life was like in Celtic times. This includes evidence for the clothes the Celts wore and the food they ate, as well as information about the Celts' tools, weapons, armour and jewellery, their homes, their transport and their religion.

A 'dig' at Maiden Castle, in Dorset. Archaeologists divide Celtic times into two periods. The first is called Hallstatt, after Hallstatt in Austria, and the second La Tène, after La Tène in Switzerland.

Everyday Life

Using evidence from their excavations, archaeologists are able to make reconstructions of Celtic houses, such as this one at Craggaunowen in County Clare, Ireland.

In Britain, most Celts lived in round houses with walls made out of stone, or upright planks of wood, or panels of wattle-and-daub. A Celtic house usually had one door and no windows. Roofs were made from a thick thatch of reeds, straw or heather, and sloped steeply so that the rain and snow would run off easily. Inside, there was just one big room in which the whole family ate and slept. The floor was beaten earth, and a fire burned in the stone hearth in the centre. As well as warming the house, the fire gave off light and heat for cooking. There was no chimney, so the smoke from the fire had to make its way out through the thatch. Around the wall there was a low bench covered with animal skins. This served as a seat by day, and a bed by night. There were also low tables for eating from, and perhaps some shelves and hooks in the wall for storing food, clothes, tools and weapons.

This painting shows what it was like inside a Celtic house at Maiden Castle, Dorset. It also shows the sort of clothes worn by the Celts. The Celts had no buttons or zips, so clothes were held together with brooches and belts.

Food and farming

The Celts grew all the food they needed in the fields around their homes. Their main cereal crops were barley, wheat, oats and rye. Grain from these crops was used to make meal for stews and porridge, and flour for bread. Some was used for brewing beer and some was saved to be planted for the next year's crop. Their vegetables included peas, beans, lentils and onions, and they kept pigs for their meat. Cattle also provided meat, together with milk and skins to make into leather. Sheep provided wool and milk, while hens and geese gave feathers and eggs. The Celts kept swarms of bees in wickerwork hives and gathered the honey to be used as a sweetener.

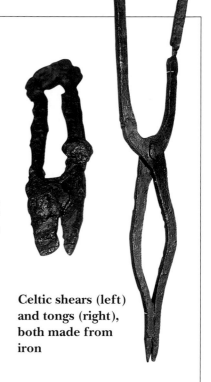

Celtic shears (left) and tongs (right), both made from iron

ares, fowl and geese they think it unlawful to eat, but rear them for pleasure and amusement.

The ground [is] thickly studded with homesteads... and the cattle very numerous.

Julius Caesar

Cooking and eating

Most food was cooked slowly over the fire in a large iron cauldron. Sometimes the cauldron stood on a tripod, or it could be hung on a chain from one of the beams in the roof. Bread was baked on a flat stone in the hearth or in a special, beehive-shaped oven made from clay. There were knives for cutting food, but no forks to eat it with. Instead, everyone used their fingers! There were very few spoons, so people mopped up gravy and other liquids with chunks of bread.

It's true!

Only small fragments of cloth survive from Celtic times. They have been buried in the ground for such a long time that they have lost their original colour. However, by studying the threads in laboratories, archaeologists can discover what dyes they contain and work out what colours they were when they were new. Archaeologists know that the Celts made their dyes from plants, using woad leaves for blue, madder root for red and the weld plant for yellow. The Celts also mixed these dyes to make green, orange, purple and brown.

A large pot found at Maiden Castle. It was probably used for storing grain or other food.

Women's work

Celtic women spent a large part of each day keeping their families fed and clothed. As well as cooking and serving meals, they had to grind enough grain into flour to make fresh bread every day. They also spent a lot of time spinning wool into yarn. The yarn was woven into cloth on a wooden handloom. When the cloth was long enough, it was taken from the loom and made into clothes for various members of the family.

Arts and crafts

The earliest Celts made their own tools, weapons, cooking utensils, pottery and simple jewellery. However, as the Celts became more successful at farming not everyone had to work on the land all the time in order to produce enough food to survive. Instead, some people were able to concentrate on arts and craftwork, making decorative and practical objects from gold, bronze, silver, iron, pottery and glass. The items they produced were then bartered for food or for other items of a similar value.

Ironwork

Iron was the most important metal for the Celts. Iron ore (rock containing iron) was found in lumps in marshes and woodlands throughout the British Isles, and it could easily be dug up. The iron ore was put into a small furnace heated by a charcoal fire. The heat of the fire melted the ore, leaving a lump of purer iron in the bottom of the furnace. This process is known as smelting. The lump of iron was then taken to the blacksmith's forge. The blacksmith heated it until it was soft, then hammered it on an anvil until it was the shape he wanted. The iron was used for practical items such as knives, swords, chains and sickles. Blacksmiths sometimes made decorative objects for the homes of the wealthy, such as ornate firedogs used to support logs in an open fire.

Part of a firedog from Welwyn in Hertfordshire (left). It was made from iron in the 1st century BC. The picture (right) shows how firedogs were used to hold logs in place in a fire.

Bronze, gold and silver

Celtic craftworkers used bronze, gold and silver to make jewellery and small statues, to decorate weapons and to make some household utensils. Bronze is a mixture of copper and tin. One method of working bronze was to melt it and then shape it into small bars, or ingots. When the ingots had cooled and set, they were hammered out into flat sheets. Craftworkers then cut the sheets of bronze and used them to strengthen wooden objects such as buckets and shields. Another method of working with bronze was to pour the molten metal into moulds to make small objects such as brooches, rings and statues. Similar methods were used for working gold and silver. These metals could also be pulled into lengths of fine wire. Craftworkers made beautiful armbands and necklaces, called torques, by twisting several of these wires together. Torques were worn by nobles and warriors.

These torques date from the 1st century BC and are made of solid gold. Two (below) were found at Ipswich in Suffolk. The other one (left) was found at Snettisham in Norfolk.

This bucket is from the 1st century BC and was found at Aylesford in Kent. It was made of wood, then decorated with bands of bronze which also helped to make it stronger.

Glass and enamel

Although the Celts did not know how to make glass for windows and large objects, they did know how to produce it in small amounts. They made glass beads and ornaments which were often patterned by adding streaks and dots of melted glass in a second colour after the first one had hardened. They also produced small amounts of enamel which was used to decorate metal objects. Their favourite colour for enamel was red, followed by yellow, green and blue.

An enamelled bronze plaque from a horse's harness. It was found in France, but was probably made in Britain in the 1st or 2nd century BC.

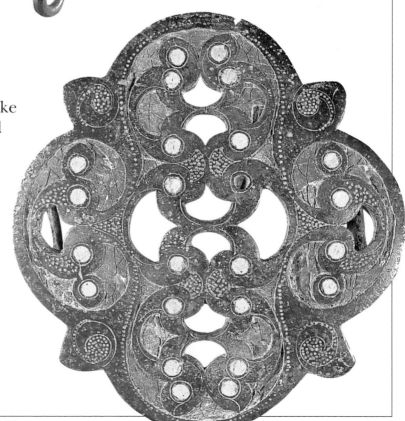

Trade and transport

Celtic tribes in Britain traded with neighbouring tribes, and also with other Celts in mainland Europe. To carry out this trade, Celtic people often made long journeys over land and sea and along lakes and rivers. They exchanged surplus goods for those they could not make themselves. They also traded raw materials which were plentiful in Britain for those which were not available. The most important of these raw materials was tin, which was found in Cornwall. The tin was exchanged for materials such as coral and amber, which were used to make jewellery and to decorate metal wine jugs and harness mounts.

Trade with the Romans

The Celts in Britain also traded with the Romans. They sent high-quality woollen cloth, hides, wool and grain to be exchanged for pottery and glassware. They also forced some people into slavery and sold them to the Romans. Slaves were often sold as payment for wine which the Celts could not make themselves. Probably very few Celts from Britain actually travelled as far as Rome. Instead, the goods probably changed hands three or four times on the journey, so that no one had to travel too far in unfamiliar territory.

Valuable items, such as this bronze flagon, were traded over long distances and used in the homes of wealthy Celts. The flagon is decorated with coral and enamel. It was found in France, but its design was influenced by the work of the Etruscans who lived in northern Italy.

They [Roman merchants] transport the wine by boat on the navigable rivers and by wagon through the plains and receive in return for it an incredibly large price; for one jar of wine they receive in return a slave, a servant in exchange for the drink.

Diodorus Siculus

Two Celtic coins with horse designs. The one on the left was made for the Catuvellauni tribe.

Iron bars and gold coins

For many years, goods were bartered for other items of similar value. Then the Celts developed a system of paying with iron bars. These bars were about 80 centimetres long. They could be used to buy goods, and to make or repair iron tools and weapons. However, by the middle of the 1st century BC, coins were in common use in most parts of Britain. Celtic coins were small and made of gold, silver or bronze. They were decorated with designs that ranged from ears of barley and vine leaves to horses and chariots, warriors, priests and bulls. Some coins were also stamped with the name of the ruler who had them made.

A coracle was made from a light wickerwork frame, with animal skins stretched tightly across the frame.

Travelling on land

The Celts were skilled horse riders and often travelled overland on horseback. In places where the ground was not too rough, they might travel in a two-wheeled chariot or a four-wheeled cart, pulled by two horses. These vehicles were made from wood and had wooden wheels with iron tyres. Journeys were often quite dangerous. It was easy to get lost, and travellers could be attacked by wild animals such as boars or wolves that lived in the forests.

Travelling on water

For journeys on rivers and lakes, the Celts used a small boat called a coracle. A coracle had a wickerwork frame with animal skins stretched over it to make it waterproof. It carried one person who paddled along with a single oar. For travelling on the sea, the Celts had larger wooden boats which could be rowed or sailed. With no maps to guide them, they had to use the sun and the stars to find their way. As a result, they usually tried to sail within sight of land, and only crossed the open sea at its narrowest points.

It's true!

Fishermen in parts of west Wales still use coracles when they go fishing in deep parts of some rivers.

Religion

Celtic religion had close connections with the forces of nature and the environment. This was because most Celts were farmers who relied on nature to make their crops grow and ripen. Without good crops, farmers and their families would go hungry.

The Celts had many different gods and goddesses. Some, such as the Earth Mother, Epona the horse goddess, and Elen the water goddess, were worshipped all over the land. Others belonged to one particular tribe or to one place, such as a pool or a spring, a tree or a stone. The Celts made sacrifices to the gods to keep them happy and to persuade them to grant favours. According to Roman writers, the Celts sometimes sacrificed people on altars in sacred groves, where oak trees and mistletoe grew. However, more usual sacrifices were gifts of flowers, or valuable objects and pieces of clothing belonging to the person asking the favour.

Following a tradition that goes back to Celtic times, people in some villages in Derbyshire and Staffordshire still decorate the local wells once a year. They make the decorative pictures from flowers.

A bronze statue of Epona, the horse goddess. It shows her feeding two ponies from a dish of corn. She was worshipped throughout the Celtic lands, but was especially popular in Britain and Gaul (France).

Druids

The Celtic religious leaders in Britain were called druids. They were the wise men of the tribe and were often political leaders, too. It took as long as 20 years to memorise all the knowledge needed to be a druid. Druids made decisions about when and where to go to war and knew all the laws relating to their tribe. They were responsible for organising the various religious ceremonies throughout the year. Some druids helped to heal the sick, partly by demanding sacrifices and partly by using herbs and medicines. Druids also decided which days of the year were lucky, and which were not.

A chariot burial at Garton-on-the-Wolds in Yorkshire. The chariot has been dismantled and its iron-rimmed wheels laid flat on the ground.

Life after death

The Celts believed that people could die and be born again many times over. They thought that after death in this world they would move on to another one which was just like it. After a certain number of years there, they would die again and then be reborn in this world.

Burials

The Celts usually buried their dead with their favourite jewellery, weapons and clothing. They believed that the dead person would need all these items on their journey to the next world. They also put food and drink in the grave including joints of meat, cauldrons, plates, large amounts of wine and cups to put it in. Wealthy Celts were sometimes buried with their chariots and horses. As these were very valuable items, the Celts made sure that they were old and worn-out before they were buried!

A grove there was, untouched by men's hands from ancient times, whose interlacing boughs enclosed a space of darkness and cold shade, and banished the sunlight from above... gods were worshipped there with savage rites, the altars were heaped with hideous offerings, and every tree was sprinkled with human gore.

Lucan, a Roman poet, describing a sacred grove in Gaul (France)

Feasts and entertainment

The Celts had four main festivals in the year. These festivals were part of the Celtic religion, and were based on important times in nature and the seasons. *Imbolc* was celebrated on 1 February, which was the start of the lambing season. This meant that the ewes had plenty of milk which could be used for making cheese. The next festival was *Beltane* at the beginning of May. This was when the cattle could be sent out to graze in the fields again, after being kept near the farm and fed on hay over the winter. Before they were sent out, two huge fires were lit outdoors and the cattle were driven between them. This was thought to protect the cattle from diseases. *Lugnasad* was the next festival. It was celebrated in August when the crops began to ripen in the fields, promising a good harvest. The final festival of the year was *Samhain*, which was celebrated on 1 November. It marked the end of one year and the start of the next, and it was the most important festival of all. It was also the time when the animals were brought back in from the fields. Those that were not needed for breeding were killed for food.

Special food and drink

After the religious parts of their festivals, the Celts enjoyed a good meal. Meat such as pork, beef, wild boar or venison would be roasted on a spit, or stewed with herbs and vegetables in a large cauldron. The meat was eaten with bread and washed down with plenty of wine or beer.

They have large quantities of food together with all kinds of meat especially fresh and salt pork.

Strabo

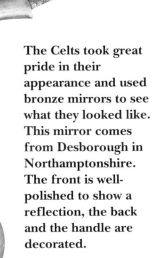

The Celts took great pride in their appearance and used bronze mirrors to see what they looked like. This mirror comes from Desborough in Northamptonshire. The front is well-polished to show a reflection, the back and the handle are decorated.

It's true!

The Celts believed that *Samhain* was a time of magic, as it belonged neither to the old year nor the new one. They thought that spirits could come into the human world and humans could go into the spirit world at this time. This was also the time when the gods played tricks on humans and demanded sacrifices before they would stop. The memory of some of this magic still survives in our Hallowe'en celebrations on 31 October.

Counters for board games have been found at many different sites. At Ravenglass in Cumbria this board was also found, but sadly there were no instructions to tell us how the game was played!

Indoor entertainment

As well as eating and drinking, the Celts played and sang music at their feasts. They accompanied their singing with flutes and lyres. Bards recited poetry and told stories about the history of the tribe and its heroes. As the evening went on, and more alcohol was drunk, boasting contests sometimes started. In these contests, each warrior tried to outdo all the others with tales of his skills in fighting and hunting.

They also invite strangers to their banquets, and only after the meal do they ask who they are and of what they stand in need.

Diodorus Siculus

[The Celts drink] a little at a time, not more than a mouthful – but they do it rather frequently.

Posidonius

When the Celts went racing, their horses and ponies sometimes wore caps to protect their heads. This cap has a hole for each ear and a third hole to carry a plume of feathers. The horns were with the cap when it was found in Scotland, but in fact they are not part of it.

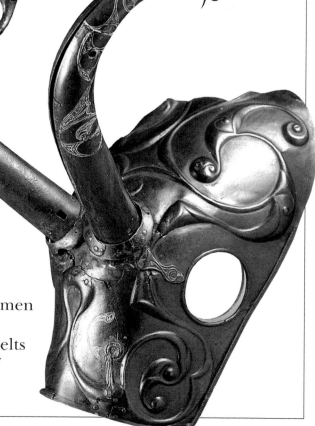

Outdoor entertainment

The summer festivals were often accompanied by horse racing and chariot racing. These events gave the young men of the tribe an opportunity to show off their skills. They were also a way of practising for possible warfare. The Celts enjoyed gambling, so they would bet on the outcome of each race.

Attack and defence

The Celts were fond of fighting. It was said that they would fight among themselves if they could not find a suitable enemy! As a result, warriors were important people in Celtic society. Most warriors were men, but occasionally women also went into battle. The most famous of these female warriors is Boudicca, who led her people against the Romans in AD 60. (You can read more about Boudicca on page 21.)

Weapons and armour

The Celts used many different weapons. Their favourite weapon was the sword. It had a long blade, made from iron, and was used for slashing at the enemy rather than stabbing. The Celts also fought with daggers, knives and battle-axes. At the start of a battle, they might throw spears or javelins at the enemy, or fire small, round stones from a sling-shot. They protected their heads with close-fitting helmets made from leather, bronze or iron. Some warriors wore chain-mail shirts, but these were very expensive and only the wealthy could afford them. Other warriors protected their bodies with tall wooden shields, which were often covered with thick leather. The handle, or boss, of the shield was usually made from iron and could be used as a weapon if the shield was cut away in the fighting.

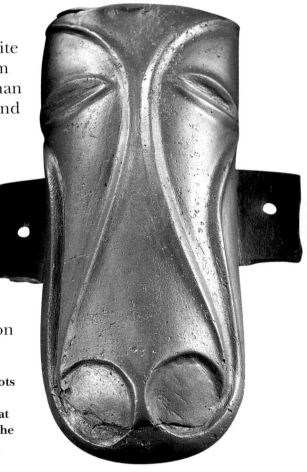

Some Celts decorated their war chariots with small metal plaques, such as this horse's head. This plaque was found at Stanwick in Yorkshire. It dates from the 1st century AD and is made of bronze.

Battle tactics

The Celts did not have organised armies or plans for fighting battles. Instead, they tried to make surprise attacks on their enemies, or scare them into giving in without a fight. If this did not work, warriors on horseback and in war chariots charged at the enemy at full speed. They were followed by the rest of the army, brandishing their weapons and blowing their war trumpets. If the enemy warriors continued to stand their ground, the Celts would fight to the death rather than admit defeat and be taken prisoner.

An aerial view of Maiden Castle, Dorset (above). Like all hill-forts, it was on top of a natural hill, but the ditches and ramparts were constructed by the Celts to make it difficult for the enemy to get inside. The painting (right) shows what Maiden Castle looked like in Celtic times.

Hill-forts, brochs and crannogs

As well as fighting their enemies, the Celts also defended their families and their property. One way of doing this was by building hill-forts into which large numbers of people could go with their animals and their belongings if they were being threatened. You can still see the outlines of these hill-forts in many places in Britain, for example at Maiden Castle in Dorset. In the north of Scotland, where there were fewer people, the Celts built tall, round towers, known as brochs. Inside, a broch had a double wall with a staircase running round it. The staircase led up to the living areas which were built on platforms jutting across the centre (see diagram). In Scotland and Ireland, houses were sometimes built on man-made islands in lakes. These were known as crannogs. They were often surrounded by a stout fence with a gatehouse to help keep unwanted intruders out.

The ruined broch at Dun Carloway on the Isle of Lewis (left). You can see clearly the remains of the double wall. The diagram (above) shows what it was like inside a broch. The walls were so high that the sun could not shine in. As a result, it was cold, dark and damp all the time.

19

The Roman conquest

Around the same time as the Celts from Hallstatt were first trading salt with the Ancient Greeks (see page 6), Rome was developing from a collection of small villages by the River Tiber into a city. Both the Celts and the Romans wanted to expand their territories and this soon brought them into conflict with each other. At first, the Celts were able to defeat the Romans. Around 390 BC, they even attacked Rome itself! However, the Roman army soon started to be better organised, and after 225 BC it defeated the Celts every time. Once this happened, the Romans began to conquer Celtic lands in mainland Europe. By 58 BC only Gaul (France) and Britain remained unconquered.

Caesar's invasions

Julius Caesar was one of Rome's most skilful soldiers. He was also ambitious, desiring both wealth and glory. In 59 BC he was put in charge of two new Roman provinces in northern Italy which had been won from the Celts. They were called Cisalpine and Transalpine Gaul. While he was there, Caesar realised that if he could conquer the whole of Gaul it would help him achieve his ambitions. Caesar's army moved into Gaul in 58 BC, and by 55 BC most of the region was under his control. In that year and the next Caesar led expeditions to Britain, but both times he failed to conquer the country.

This map shows how Caesar and his army conquered Gaul (France), starting in the southeast and gradually moving to the north and west.

After Caesar's expeditions to Britain, the Romans tried to spread their influence by trading with the Celts. They traded luxury goods, such as this silver pepper-pot which is made to look like a fashionable Roman woman. The Romans thought that the wealth of their empire would impress the Celts so much that they would want to be part of it.

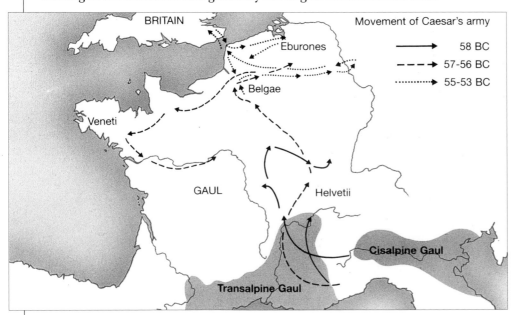

Claudius invades Britain

After the Roman victory over Gaul, the British kept up their links with the Celts who lived there. They traded with them and with the Romans, too. The British also continued to fight among themselves, making some Celtic leaders in Britain think that they might be better off if the Romans were there to protect them. In AD 43, one of these leaders went to the Roman emperor, Claudius, to ask for his help. He wanted to defeat the tribe of Catuvellauni who were led by Caratacus. Claudius saw this as a good excuse to invade Britain and sent an army of 50,000 men to do the job for him. The Romans landed near Richborough in Kent and fought their way inland until they reached Colchester, which was the capital of the Catuvellauni. Eleven Celtic leaders surrendered to the Romans there, and soon the invaders controlled the whole country to the south and east of a line from Exeter to Lincoln.

Rebellion

Although the Romans conquered the lowlands of Britain easily, they found the hilly areas more difficult. From about AD 49 they tried to conquer Wales. Caratacus had fled there from Colchester and led many attacks on the Romans. This kept the Roman army busy until AD 51, when Caratacus was betrayed by Cartimandua, the queen of the Brigantes. Then, in eastern Britain, another Celtic queen rebelled against the Romans. Her name was Boudicca and she was angry about the way the Romans had treated her people, the Iceni. Her tribe joined forces with the Trinovantes and in AD 60 they burned down the Roman towns of Camulodunum (Colchester), Verulamium (St Albans) and Londinium (London) before they were defeated.

Roman soldiers were well-armed and well-organised. They practised their battle tactics and fought as a team.

They dye their skin with woad which makes them blue, and they look more terrifying in battle.

Julius Caesar, writing about the Celts

The Romans built walls around their towns to protect them from attackers and to control trade. The remains of these Roman walls are at Colchester.

As the Romans became more settled in Britain, they began to build places for entertainment. The ruins of this amphitheatre can be seen at Verulamium (St Albans).

Roman Britain

Once the Romans had put down Boudicca's rebellion and rebuilt the towns that had been destroyed, they set out to try and conquer the rest of Britain. Some tribes fought against the Romans, but others accepted them. This made it easier for the Romans to squash any further rebellions and bring southern Britain more firmly under their control.

A changing landscape

The Romans began to make great changes to the landscape of Britain. Where the Celts had built with wood and thatch, the Romans used stones or bricks and roofed their buildings with tiles. They laid paved roads which ran in straight lines so that armies, messengers and supplies could move quickly from one place to another. They built army camps and then permanent forts for the legions of Roman soldiers who occupied the country. The soldiers needed somewhere to live when they were not on duty, so the Romans began to build new towns. These towns were carefully planned, with two main streets crossing at right angles in the centre. They all had a forum (market place), a basilica (town hall), temples, shops, public baths, taverns, a theatre and an amphitheatre, as well as houses, public lavatories, a water supply and a sewage system. With all these facilities, the towns began to attract the Celts, and soon many of them adopted a Roman way of life.

This map shows roads, towns and forts in Roman Britain in the middle of the 2nd century AD.

□ main forts
• towns

Antonine Wall
Hadrian's Wall
Housesteads Fort
York
Chester
Lincoln
Caistor
Norwich
Wroxeter
Leicester
Colchester
Gloucester
St Albans
Caerleon
Cirencester
London
Richbo
Bath
Silchester
Lullingstone Villa
Exeter
Portchester

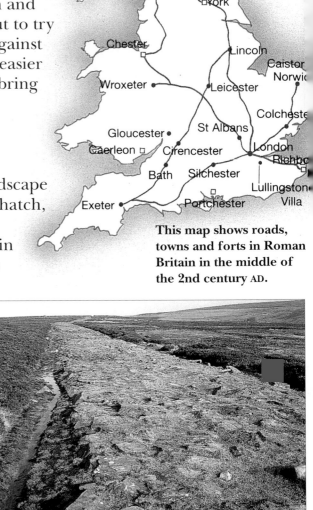

This stretch of Roman road can still be seen on Wheeldale Moor in Yorkshire. As well as being paved, it has drainage channels on both sides.

Part of the villa at Lullingstone in Kent. Like all villas in Britain, Lullingstone was very spacious.

Housesteads Fort on Hadrian's Wall, as seen from the air. As well as the rows of barracks for the soldiers, the fort had granaries, storerooms and a hospital.

The northern frontier

The Romans kept trying to push the frontier of their empire northwards, but they did not have much success. Then in AD 122 the Emperor Hadrian visited Britain. He gave orders for a wall to be built across the country between the rivers Solway and Tyne. This was to stop the Picts and other northern tribes from attacking the rest of Britain. When it was completed, Hadrian's Wall was 120 kilometres long and had 16 major forts. Twenty years later, the Romans tried to push their frontier further north again by building the Antonine Wall between the rivers Clyde and Forth. However, they had problems supplying enough soldiers to patrol the area. After only 20 years the Antonine Wall was abandoned.

It's true!

The Romans wanted to take control of Britain because of its natural wealth. There were large reserves of tin and iron as well as lead, silver and gold. British sheep provided good wool for making cloth, and there were plenty of cattle to supply skins for leather.

What happened to the Celts?

Some Celts joined the Roman army, where they were especially valued as cavalrymen. Others became rich through trading with the Romans in Britain. Many carried on farming as they had done before, but built themselves Roman-style houses or villas to live in. Some did not want to live in an occupied country and follow a Roman way of life, and so they moved north or west to the areas where there was little or no Roman influence.

This 2nd-century bowl was found in London. Pottery such as this was made in Gaul (France) and used in all parts of Roman Britain.

Celtic Christianity

When the Romans invaded Britain, they brought with them their own gods and goddesses. These included Mercury, Venus, Diana, Jupiter, Pluto and Mars. The Romans built temples to these gods, but they also allowed the Celts to continue worshipping their own gods and goddesses. However, the Romans banned the activities of the druids, because they thought the druids' teachings threatened Roman rule in Britain.

The first Christians

At the start of the 3rd century AD, a new religion began to spread across Britain. This religion was Christianity. It was probably brought to the country by soldiers and traders travelling from other parts of the Roman Empire. Christians believed that there was only one god. The Romans believed in many traditional gods, and that their emperors became gods when they died. Because of this difference in beliefs, the Romans persecuted the Christians for many years. Then in AD 312 the Roman emperor, Constantine, became a Christian. Constantine made Christianity the official religion of his empire.

After the Romans

The last of the Roman armies left Britain in AD 402 to go and defend Rome from attacks by barbarian tribes. At the same time, eastern Britain was invaded by Angles, Jutes and Saxons (see page 26) who were looking for new lands to settle. These people brought their own religions with them, but Christianity survived among the Celts in the west.

Saint Patrick

The man we know as Saint Patrick was born on the west coast of Britain in around AD 385. He was the grandson of a Christian priest, but when he was about 16 years old he was captured by pirates and taken to Ireland as a slave. He managed to escape to France where he trained to be a Christian priest. He then went back to Ireland and started converting the Irish people to Christianity.

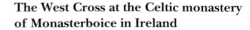

The West Cross at the Celtic monastery of Monasterboice in Ireland

 Words, words, words

In Wales there are many place names beginning with the word 'Llan', which means 'church' in English. Many of these places are the sites of very early Celtic churches.

Celtic saints and monasteries

Saint Patrick persuaded some of his followers to set up monasteries where monks could spend time praying and studying the Bible. The monks supported themselves by farming, and they looked after the old, the sick and the poor. By the end of the 5th century AD, there were also Celtic monasteries in Wales and Cornwall.

Some monks went out to convert other people to Christianity. One of the most successful was Saint Columba. He left Ireland and founded a monastery on Iona, from where much of Scotland was converted. Another was Saint David who founded many churches in Wales in the 6th century. Then in the 7th century, Saint Aidan left Iona and founded a monastery at Lindisfarne, off the coast of Northumbria. He worked from Lindisfarne to convert people in northern England to Christianity.

Celtic metalworkers made beautiful objects for their churches. This silver chalice comes from Ardagh, Ireland. It was made around AD 700.

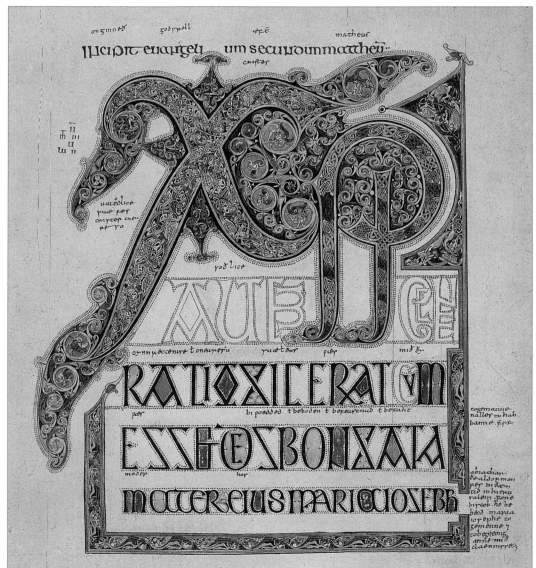

It's true!

In AD 664 there was a great meeting at Whitby, in northeast England, between the leaders of the Celtic and the Roman churches. Although both churches were Christian, they had some different ideas about how they should be organised. After much talk, the Celtic Christians finally agreed to join the Romans, and accept the Pope as their leader.

A page from the Lindisfarne Gospels. It took many weeks to produce a page like this, with its many colours and swirling patterns.

Celtic survival

In mainland Europe, most Celts quickly adopted Roman ways after their lands became part of the Roman Empire. But in Britain the situation was rather different. There were large areas of Britain where the Romans had little or no influence, and in these places the Celtic ways of life were able to survive for many more centuries.

Celts on the move

After the Romans left Britain, the Angles, Jutes and Saxons began to invade and settle. These invaders came from the region that is present-day Denmark and northern Germany. They brought their families with them to Britain, and set up farms in the south and the east of the country. At the same time, Celts from Ireland moved into the west of Britain and settled there. The tribe known as the Scotti settled down in the north and gave their name to the land we now call Scotland. Other Celts lived in the areas of Wales now called Gwynedd and Dyfed, and from there they invaded Devon and Cornwall. Meanwhile, Celts from South-west Britain moved to Brittany in France, taking with them their language and customs.

Words, words, words

The Anglo-Saxons used the word 'Welsh' to describe all the Celts. Places in England which have the word 'wal' in their names are probably places where some Celts continued to live after the Angles and Saxons arrived.

This map shows the many migrations which took place in and around Britain after the Roman army left at the start of the 5th century AD.

Scotti

Jutes

An

Saxons

Gwynedd

Dyfed

Devon

Cornwall

Brittany

Words, words, words

The British Celts called themselves 'Cymry' which means 'fellow countrymen'. The word still survives today in the name of Cumbria in northwest England. It also survives in the Welsh name for Wales, Cymru.

Some Irish monks built tall, round towers in which they could hide with their treasures when the Vikings came. This tower is at Glendalough in County Wicklow.

A modern pendant and a brooch use traditional Celtic patterns in their design.

Celts in danger

From the 9th century the Celts in Scotland and Ireland had to face a new threat from Viking raiders attacking their coasts. The Vikings robbed many monasteries of their treasures, and took the monks away to be sold into slavery. Some monks built tall, round towers in which they could shelter with their precious belongings until the raiders had gone.

Not all the Vikings were intent on raiding. Some settled in eastern England, and around the edges of Scotland and Ireland. Many wanted to trade, and they set up trading centres at places such as Dublin, Wexford, Waterford and Cork. Other Vikings formed alliances with various Irish chieftains who were often at war with each other. In 1014, Brian Boru, the High King of Ireland, defeated the Vikings at the battle of Clontarf. After this date, Viking power in Ireland began to decline.

Language, arts and crafts

Over the centuries, the old Celtic ways of life gradually disappeared, but many of the languages, arts and crafts lived on. In the 20th century, many people in Celtic areas have begun to take pride in their Celtic inheritance. Celtic languages such as Welsh, Gaelic, Erse and Breton are once more widely spoken in Wales, Scotland, Ireland and Brittany, but Cornish and Manx (the language of the Isle of Man) have died out. Designs in jewellery and metalwork which were popular with the early Celts are still used to decorate objects today.

Words, words, words

The names of many rivers in England are of Celtic origin. They include the Severn, the Dove, the Swale and the Avon. Some hills also have Celtic names. Two of the best known are Pen-y-Ghent in Yorkshire, and Pendle in Lancashire.

After a lot of campaigning by Welsh people, most road signs in Wales are now written in both Welsh and English.

Myths and Legends

Apart from their languages and their influence on arts and crafts, the other great survival from Celtic times is a wealth of myths and legends, mainly from Wales and Ireland.

Celtic writing

In Europe, Celtic alphabets were based on the alphabets used by other people. This varied from place to place, depending who the Celts had most contact with. However, the Celts in Britain developed their own alphabets independently. The Ogham alphabet was used mainly in Ireland and western Britain. It had 25 letters, all made up of straight lines. Another alphabet used in Wales had 30 letters.

While the druids were in power, they allowed very few people to learn to read or write as they thought this might threaten their power. This meant that stories were passed on by word of mouth from one generation to the next. But from the 6th century onwards, Celtic myths and legends were written down by Christian monks. These monks also made beautiful, handwritten and decorated copies of the Bible and other religious books.

The first page of St Mark's Gospel from the Book of Durrow, produced by monks in Ireland around AD 680

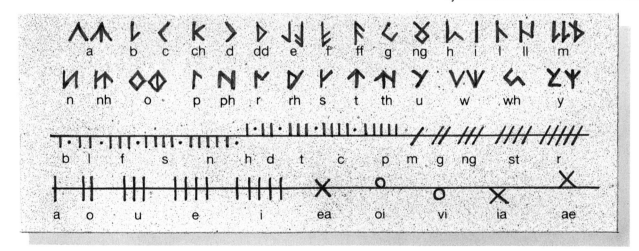

A Welsh alphabet (top) and the Ogham alphabet (below). The letters of the Celtic alphabets were made up of straight lines. This was because they were usually carved into stone or wood where curves would have been difficult to cut.

The Welsh legends

The main collection of Welsh Celtic legends is known as the *Mabinogion*, although it was not given this title until the 19th century. The *Mabinogion* contains 11 stories, the first four of which feature Pryderi, an early prince of Dyfed. Five of the others are about King Arthur, but Merlin the Magician is a later invention.

Legends from Ireland

The biggest collection of Celtic legends comes from Ireland. These legends tell tales of the old Celtic gods and goddesses, as well as of humans and animals. Most of them are grouped into three collections, or cycles. The first of these is known as the *Mythological Cycle* and tells of two battles between two armies of supernatural beings who invade Ireland. The second one is the *Ulster Cycle* which tells the story of Cú Chulainn, a hero who has magical powers. The third is the *Fenian Cycle*, which is sometimes also known as the *Ossian Cycle*. It tells the story of Finn MacCool and his son Oisin (also known as Ossian). Their followers are known as the Fianna or Fenians.

The name Cú Chulainn means 'the hound of Culann'. This name was given to the hero of the *Ulster Cycle* after he killed Culann the Smith's guard dog which attacked him at a feast. He offered to act as Culann's guard until another suitable dog could be trained.

What the legends tell us today

The Welsh and Irish legends have all been translated into English and can still be read today. As well as being good stories, they are very useful for giving us clues about the way the Celts looked at life and what they believed. But the stories are not true accounts of what happened in Celtic times. To find out about the Celts, we have to rely on the work of archaeologists who study objects left behind by the Celts, and build up a picture of Celtic life from their findings.

Is it true?

The most famous character in Celtic legend is King Arthur. He was a Christian king who fought against the invading Saxons after the Romans had left Britain. He was helped by a company of knights and a magician called Merlin. Stories about him became very popular in Europe in the Middle Ages. There probably really was a British leader called Arthur, but it is very unlikely that the rest of the legend is true.

King Arthur's Round Table in the Great Hall of Winchester Castle was probably made no earlier than the 13th century AD!

Index

Glossary

archaeologist   someone who makes a scientific study of the past, often by digging up objects in the ground

bard   the Celtic name for a poet or a story-teller

barter   to obtain goods by exchanging them for other goods rather than buying them with money

basilica   a public building in the centre of a Roman town. It was rather like a modern-day town hall

Brigantes   the name of a Celtic tribe who lived in and around the Pennines in what is now Yorkshire

broch   the name given to the round towers built for defence by the Celts in the north of Scotland

charcoal   pieces of wood which have been charred, or roasted, before being used for fuel

coracle   a small boat made out of a wickerwork frame covered with animal skins

crannog   a house built on a man-made island in lakes in Scotland and Ireland

druid   a Celtic religious leader in Britain

enamel   a hard shiny substance used for decorating metal objects. Enamel was made by heating a mixture of quartz glass and lead until it melted. Different colours could be added to it

forum   an open area in the centre of a Roman town. Markets and political meetings were held there

furnace   an enclosed fire which burned at a high temperature and was used for melting metal from ore

Gaul   the Celtic name for present-day France

Iceni   the name of a Celtic tribe who lived in what is now East Anglia

ingot   a bar of solid metal which can be melted down or hammered into shape

legion   a division of the Roman army. A legion was about 6000 men

lyre   an ancient stringed instrument. The strings were plucked to make music

ore   rock that contains a metal, for example iron

sickle   a cutting tool with a curved metal blade and a short wooden handle. It was used to harvest crops

sling-shot   a little catapult used to fire round stones

smelting   the process of extracting metal from its ore by heating in a furnace

thatch   a roof covering made up of a thick layer of reeds, straw or heather

tripod   a three-legged device from which a cauldron could be hung over a fire

venison   deer meat

wattle-and-daub   panels of interwoven twigs plastered with mud and used to build houses

Places to visit

Museums

The British Museum, London
The National Museum of Ireland, Dublin
The National Museum of Scotland, Edinburgh
The National Museum of Wales, Cardiff
Ashmolean Museum, Oxford
City Museum and Art Gallery, Gloucester
Colchester Museum, Essex
Devizes Museum, Devizes, Wiltshire
Dorset County Museum, Dorchester, Dorset
Hull and East Riding Museum, Hull, Yorkshire
Lewes Museum, Lewes, East Sussex
Museum of Archaeology and Ethnography, Cambridge
Museum of the Iron Age, Andover, Hampshire
Northamptonshire Museum, Northampton
Red House Museum, Christchurch, Dorset
Salisbury Museum, Salisbury, Wiltshire
Somerset County Museum, Taunton, Somerset
The Yorkshire Museum, York
Welsh Folk Museum, St Fagans, Cardiff, Glamorganshire
    – reconstruction of a Celtic village

Sites

England
Butser Hill, Hampshire – reconstruction of a Celtic village
Caer Caradoc, Shropshire – hill-fort
Chysauster, Cornwall – village with courtyard and houses
Danebury Hill-fort, Hampshire
Eddisbury Hill-fort, Cheshire
Eggardon Hill-fort, Dorset
Hod Hill, Dorset – hill-fort
Humbledon Hill, Northumberland – hill-fort
Ingleborough, North Yorkshire – hill-fort
Maiden Castle, Dorset – hill-fort
Old Oswestry, Shropshire – hill-fort
Uffington Castle, Oxfordshire – figure of white horse

Ireland
Baltinglass Hill, Co. Wicklow – hill-fort
Caherconell, Co. Clare – stone fort
Craggaunowen, Co. Clare – reconstruction of a crannog
Dun Aillinne, Co. Kildare – hill-fort
Rathgall, Co. Wicklow – hill-fort
Staigue, Co. Kerry – stone fort
Tara, Co. Meath – hill-fort
The King's Stables, Co. Armagh – ritual pool
Turoe Stone, Co. Galway – boulder with Celtic carvings

Scotland
Burnswark Hill-fort, Dumfries and Galloway
Clickhimin Broch, Mainland, Shetland
Dun Carloway Broch, Lewis
Eildon Hill, Borders – hill-fort
Gurness Broch, Mainland, Orkney
Hownam Rings, Borders – hill-fort
Kenmore, Loch Tay, Perthshire – reconstruction of a crannog
Mousa Broch, Mainland, Shetland
Traprain Law, Lothian – hill-fort

Wales
Bulwark Hill-fort, West Glamorgan
Castell Hewlys, Pembrokeshire Coast National Park – hill-fort
Carn Goch Hill-fort, Dyfed
Ffridd Faldwyn, Powys – hill-fort
Moel Arthur, Clwyd – hill-fort
Moel-y-Gaer, Rhosesmor, Clwyd – hill-fort
Tre'r Ceiri, Gwynedd – hill-fort